perfect
Pies

perfect Pies

LORENZ BOOKS

This edition published by Lorenz Books
an imprint of
Anness Publishing Limited
Hermes House, 88-89 Blackfriars Road, London SE1 8HA

This edition distributed in Canada by Raincoast Books
8680 Cambie Street, Vancouver, British Columbia V6P 6M9

ISBN 0-7548-0351-1

A CIP catalogue for this book is available from the British Library

Publisher Joanna Lorenz
Senior Cookery Editor Linda Fraser
Assistant Editor Emma Brown
Copy Editor Jenni Fleetwood
Designer Lilian Lindblom
Illustrator Anna Koska
Photographers Karl Adamson, Michael Michaels, James Duncan, Steve Baxter, Amanda Heywood,
Michelle Garrett, Patrick McLeavey, John Freeman & Edward Allwright
Recipes Christine France, Roz Denny, Patricia Lousada, Alex Barker, Sue Maggs, Liz Trigg, Rosamund
Grant, Soheila Kimberley, Frances Cleary, Elizabeth Wolf-Cohen, Jenny Stacey, Andi Clevely, Katherine
Richmond, Hilaire Walden, Shirley Gill & Norma MacMillan

For all recipes, quantities are given in both metric and imperial measures, and, where
appropriate, measures are also given in standard cups and spoons. Follow one set, but
not a mixture, because they are not interchangeable.

Also published as *The Little Pie Cookbook*

Printed and bound in Singapore

1 3 5 7 9 10 8 6 4 2

Contents

Introduction

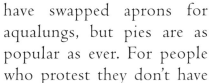

What could be nicer than a fruit pie, all golden crust and juicy fruit? Perhaps a steak and kidney pie, rich and mellow on a chilly winter's day? Or a melt-in-the-mouth mince pie, so good you reach for a second before the crumbs of the first have been brushed from your lips? And then there's filo: layers of crisp perfection topping a creamy cheese filling with tender chicken chunks. The list is as long as you choose to make it. Dreaming about one pie triggers thoughts of another, and all are bound up with other memories: grandmothers with floury elbows rolling out pastry with the ease of long practice; children shaping grubby bits of dough into their initials; hot pies cooling on window-sills; burned tongues when the jam was too hot.

Times may have changed, grannies may have swapped aprons for aqualungs, but pies are as popular as ever. For people who protest they don't have time to make pastry after a hard day at the office or taking care of the family, there is always the option of making up batches of rubbed-in mixture at moments of leisure and freezing them for later use. Every supermarket stocks frozen pastry, which is a boon to the busy cook. Few of us choose to make our own puff pastry, except for special occasions, but before you reach for the pack of frozen shortcrust, consider how simple that pastry is to make.

For some reason, inexperienced cooks get nervous about making pastry. They imagine it to be some mysterious process that takes years to master. No one would suggest puff pastry is easy, but anyone can make shortcrust. And no, you don't have to hold your hands in the freezer before you start — unless the day is very hot or you are running a fever, you are unlikely to melt the fat when rubbing in. If you are worried, run your hands briefly under the cold tap. The trick with shortcrust pastry is not to mess it about. Measuring everything carefully is important, but then you can relax a little. Rub the fat into the flour quickly, aiming for a good distribution but not perfect graded grains. Just try to avoid any pieces of fat being bigger than pea-size. Use the smallest amount of cold water you can get away with; just enough to bind the ingredients together. Soggy dough makes tough pastry. Don't knead pastry unless the recipe specifically says you should, but do let it rest in the fridge if you have time, as this relaxes the gluten and makes shrinkage less likely. Let the pastry come to room temperature before use.

As for rolling out, all it takes is even pressure and a light touch. Don't overdo the flour on the surface or the pastry will be tough; instead, lift it frequently and move it around (without turning it over). The rules suggest rolling in one direction only, but if you slip up, it won't ruin your pie, or your reputation.

Of course, not all pies involve pastry. Mashed potato makes a delicious topping, especially when mixed with parsnip, as the recipe for Farmhouse Venison Pie amply illustrates. For a sweet pie try a streusel topping: just strew crumble mixture over a fruit filling before baking for a deliciously different texture and taste.

Types of Pastry

FILO

This traditional Greek pastry comes ready rolled in paper-thin sheets, which are layered, then cooked until crisp. Filo is made with very little fat, so each layer must be brushed with oil or melted butter. It dries out quickly when exposed to the air, so any pastry not in use should be kept covered with a clean damp dish towel. Bake the filo pie as soon as it is assembled.

PUFF PASTRY

This delectable pastry is made in such a way that it separates into crisp, melt-in-the-mouth layers when cooked, thanks to air trapped in the pastry. A block of butter is wrapped in a basic dough; the pastry is then turned, rolled, folded and chilled several times. Although some cooks continue to prepare their own puff pastry, many prefer to buy it ready-made and frozen. Thaw slowly (see package instructions).

FLAKY PASTRY

Similar to puff pastry, but easier to prepare, this involves making a dough with half the stipulated amount of butter, then softening the rest to the same consistency as the dough and dotting some of it all over the surface of the rolled out rectangle of pastry. The pastry is folded, turned and rolled and the process repeated. When the pastry is baked in a hot oven it separates into crisp leaves that are beautifully light.

ROUGH PUFF

The easiest flaky pastry of all: the diced fat is mixed with the flour but not rubbed in, so that when the liquid is added a dough is formed in which the fat can be seen. The pastry is rolled and folded several times before being rested and baked. The fat for rough puff pastry should be very cold and it is helpful if the flour is chilled before use.

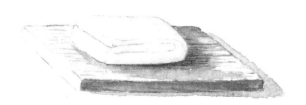

SHORTCRUST

One of the easiest of pastries, shortcrust consists of flour and fat, with just enough liquid to bind the ingredients together. The standard recipe is to sift 175g/6oz/1½ cups plain flour and a pinch of salt into a bowl, then rub in 75g/3oz/6 tbsp diced butter or solid block margarine (see Techniques, pages 10–11). Drizzle 30–45ml/2–3 tbsp iced water over the surface, then quickly fork it through until the pastry clumps together and can be shaped to a ball. If time permits, wrap shortcrust pastry in clear film and chill it for 30 minutes before rolling it out.

RICH SHORTCRUST

Richer than plain shortcrust, this sets to a crisper crust. It is often used for fruit pies. Use the standard shortcrust recipe but make with 115g/4oz/8 tbsp butter and substitute an egg yolk for part of the liquid. For a sweet pastry, add 10–15ml/2–3 tbsp caster sugar after rubbing in the fat.

COOK'S TIPS

To make a quick all-in-one pastry using tub margarine, cream 115g/4oz/½ cup tub margarine with 25g/1oz/¼ cup plain flour and 15ml/1 tbsp cold water. Add a further 150g/5oz/1¼ cups plain flour and a pinch of salt and work to a smooth dough. Wrap and chill before use.

Make up a batch of rubbed-in mixture for shortcrust pastry (without adding any liquid), put it in a tub and store it in the freezer. Next time you want to make a pie, just thaw, add water and roll out.

If you prefer to use wholemeal flour, but find it makes your pastry rather chewy, use half wholemeal and half plain flour.

Spicy pastry is perfect for apple pie. Make a rich shortcrust, but add 5ml/1 tsp each of ground allspice and cinnamon for every 115g/4oz/1 cup flour.

Techniques

RUBBING IN

Add the diced fat to the flour. Using just the tips of your fingers and thumbs, draw up a small amount of mixture and rub together to break it down into crumbs. Repeat the process, lifting the mixture each time to incorporate air, until no large lumps of fat remain. Do not overwork the dough: the perfect mixture will look like fine breadcrumbs with some larger pieces of fat (about the size of peas) dotted through it.

USING A PASTRY BLENDER

A pastry blender is a gadget comprising 5–8 arched wires on a wooden handle. Some cooks prefer it for rubbing in as it stops warm hands softening the fat too much, but it can break down the fat almost too efficiently. Use the blender for half the fat, and add the rest in pea-size pieces.

ROLLING OUT

Lightly dust a clean, level surface – and a rolling pin – with flour. Pat the pastry to a shape that echoes the shape of your dish. Using a light, even touch, roll out the pastry in one direction only (away from you), lifting the pin for the return journey. Never turn the pastry over during rolling.

CRIMPING A PASTRY SHELL

The easiest way to crimp the rim of a pastry shell is to make a 'V' of the forefinger and second finger of your right hand, pressing down lightly on the pastry. Then use the index finger of your left hand to push the pastry between the 'V' inwards. Or press the knuckle of one hand against the inner edge as shown below, using the other hand to pinch the dough around your finger into a 'V'. Continue right around the rim.

MAKING A PASTRY LATTICE

Cut long strips of pastry, about 1cm/½in wide. Keeping them an even distance apart, arrange them over the pie in a grid, either placing the vertical strips over horizontal ones, or interweaving them. The strips can also be twisted for a rustic look.

GLAZING

For a rich, golden crust, brush the pastry before baking with beaten egg, or a mixture of beaten egg and water. Alternatively, use milk. Glaze the pie just before baking it. For a sweet pie you can add a light dusting of caster sugar.

11

CUT-OUTS

Roll out a pastry lid, then cut out shapes using pastry cutters, trying not to distort the pastry. Fit the lid over the filled pastry shell. Alternatively, cut decorative shapes such as leaves from pastry trimmings and attach them to a lid with a dot of beaten egg or milk. Next time you bake a friend's favourite pie, pick out their name on it in pastry letters. The same technique can be used to identify individual pies when you are batch-baking.

BAKING BLIND

This refers to the act of partially or fully baking an unfilled pastry case. Line the pastry case with non-stick baking paper and add an even layer of baking beans (use dried beans kept especially for the purpose or special china beans). Bake for 10 minutes, then remove the paper and beans and return the pastry case to the oven for 5 minutes more, or longer if it is not to be cooked again. When cool, store the beans in a jar.

Meat Pies

Greek Lamb Pie

INGREDIENTS

sunflower oil, for brushing
450g / 1lb lean minced lamb
1 medium onion, sliced
1 garlic clove, crushed
400g / 14oz can plum tomatoes
30ml / 2 tbsp chopped fresh mint
5ml / 1 tsp grated nutmeg
350g / 12oz young spinach leaves
275g / 10oz packet filo pastry
5ml / 1 tsp sesame seeds
salt and ground black pepper

SERVES 4

1 Preheat the oven to 200°C/400°F/Gas 6. Lightly oil a 23cm/9in round springform tin.

2 Fry the mince and onion without fat in a non-stick pan until golden. Add the garlic, tomatoes, mint, nutmeg, salt and pepper. Bring to the boil, stirring. Simmer, stirring occasionally, until most of the liquid has evaporated.

3 Wash the spinach and remove any tough stalks. Place the wet leaves in a saucepan, cover and cook for about 2 minutes, until wilted.

4 Lightly brush each sheet of filo pastry with oil and lay in overlapping layers in the tin, leaving enough overhanging to wrap over the top.

5 Spoon in the meat and spinach. Wrap the pastry over to enclose the filling; scrunch it slightly. Sprinkle with sesame seeds and bake the lamb filo pie for about

25–30 minutes, or until golden and crisp. Serve the pie hot, using a sharp knife to cut through the filo.

13

Pennsylvania Dutch Ham & Apple Pie

INGREDIENTS

5 cooking apples
60ml/4 tbsp soft light brown sugar
15ml/1 tbsp plain flour
4ml/¾ tsp ground cloves
4ml/¾ tsp ground black pepper
175g/6oz sliced baked ham
25g/1oz/2 tbsp butter or margarine
60ml/4 tbsp whipping cream
1 egg yolk
PASTRY
225g/8oz/2 cups plain flour
2.5ml/½ tsp salt
75g/3oz/6 tbsp cold butter, cut in pieces
50g/2oz/4 tbsp cold margarine, cut in pieces
50–120ml/2-4fl oz/¼-½ cup iced water

SERVES 6–8

1 To make the crust, sift the flour and salt into a bowl. Rub in the butter and margarine until the mixture resembles coarse crumbs. Stir in enough water to bind, gather the dough into two balls, and wrap in clear film. Chill for 20 minutes. Preheat the oven to 220°C/425°F/Gas 7.

2 Quarter, core, peel, and thinly slice the apples. Place in a bowl and toss with the sugar, flour, cloves and pepper, to coat evenly. Set aside.

3 Roll out one dough ball 3mm/⅛in thick. Fit in a 25cm/10in pie dish. Leave an overhang.

4 Arrange half the ham slices in the bottom. Top with a layer of apple slices. Dot with half the butter or margarine. Repeat layering, finishing with apples. Dot with butter or margarine. Pour over 45ml/3 tbsp of the whipping cream, in an even layer.

5 Roll out the remaining dough and put on top of the pie. Fold the top edge under the bottom crust and press to seal. Roll out the dough scraps and stamp out decorative shapes. Arrange on top of the pie. Crimp the edge using your finger and a fork. Cut steam vents at regular intervals. Mix the egg yolk and remaining cream and brush on top of the pie to glaze. Avoid clogging the steam vents.

6 Bake for about 10 minutes. Reduce the heat to 180°C/350°F/Gas 4. Bake for 30–35 minutes more, until golden. Serve hot.

14

Steak, Kidney & Mushroom Pie

INGREDIENTS

30ml/2 tbsp oil
1 onion, chopped
115g/4oz rindless streaky bacon, chopped
500g/1¼lb chuck steak, diced
30ml/2 tbsp plain flour
115g/4oz lamb's kidneys
large bouquet garni
400ml/14fl oz/1¾ cups beef stock
175g/6oz/1½ cups button mushrooms
225g/8oz puff pastry, thawed if frozen
salt and ground black pepper
beaten egg, to glaze

SERVES 4

1 Preheat the oven to 160°C/325°F/Gas 3. Heat the oil in a heavy-based pan, then cook the onion and bacon until lightly browned.

2 Toss the steak in the flour. Stir the meat into the pan in batches and cook, stirring, until browned.

3 Toss the kidneys in flour and add to the pan with the bouquet garni. Pour in the stock, transfer to a casserole, fit the lid and cook in the oven for 2 hours. Stir in the mushrooms and seasoning and set the casserole aside to cool completely.

4 Preheat the oven to 220°C/425°F/Gas 7. Roll out the pastry to 2cm/¾in larger than the top of a 1.2 litre/2 pint/5 cup pie dish. Cut off a narrow strip from the pastry and fit around the dampened rim of the dish. Brush the pastry strip with water.

5 Tip the meat mixture into the dish. Lay the pastry over the dish, press the edges to seal, then crimp them and knock them up with the back of a knife. Make a small slit in the pastry, brush with beaten egg and bake for 20 minutes. Lower the oven temperature to 180°C/350°F/Gas 4 and bake for 20 minutes more, until the pastry is golden.

Bacon & Egg Pie

INGREDIENTS

*450-500g/1-1¼lb shortcrust pastry, thawed
if frozen
30ml/2 tbsp oil
4 rindless smoked bacon rashers, cut in
4cm/1½in pieces
1 small onion, finely chopped
5 eggs
25ml/1½ tbsp chopped fresh parsley (optional)
salt and ground black pepper
beaten egg or milk, to glaze*

SERVES 4

18

1 Use two-thirds of the pastry to line a 20cm/8in flan ring. Chill for 20 minutes. Pre-heat the oven to 200°C/400°F/ Gas 6. Heat the oil in a pan and fry the bacon and onion until the onion is soft, and the bacon is starting to crisp. Drain on kitchen paper.

2 Cover the bottom of the pastry case with the bacon mixture, spreading it evenly, then break the eggs on to the bacon, spacing them evenly apart. Carefully tilt the flan tin so the egg whites flow together. Sprinkle the eggs with the chopped fresh parsley, if using, plenty of black pepper, and just a little salt if the bacon is very salty. Place a baking sheet in the oven to heat.

3 Roll out the remaining pastry, dampen the edges and place over the filling. Press to seal the edges, then remove excess pastry and use for pastry leaves. Decorate the pie, brush it with egg or milk and make a hole in the centre.

4 Place the pie on the baking sheet and bake for 10 minutes, then reduce the oven temperature to 180°C/350°F/Gas 4 and bake for 20 minutes. Leave to cool before cutting.

Squab Pie

INGREDIENTS

675g/1½lb lamb neck fillets, cut in
12 pieces
115g/4oz gammon, diced
1 onion, thinly sliced
1 large cooking apple, peeled, cored and sliced
350g/12oz leeks, sliced
1.5-2.5ml/¼-½ tsp ground allspice
1.5-2.5ml/¼-½ tsp freshly grated nutmeg
150ml/¼ pint/¾ cup lamb, beef or
vegetable stock
225g/8oz shortcrust pastry, thawed if frozen
salt and ground black pepper
beaten egg or milk, to glaze

SERVES 4

19

1 Preheat the oven to 200°C/400°F/Gas 6. Layer the lamb, gammon, onion, apple and the leeks in a 900ml/1½ pint/3¾ cup pie dish, sprinkling in the spices and seasoning as you go. Pour in the lamb, beef or vegetable stock to moisten the mixture.

2 Roll out the pastry to 2cm/¾in larger than the top of the pie dish. Cut a narrow strip from around the pastry, fit it around the dampened rim of the dish, then brush with water.

3 Lay the pastry over the dish and crimp the edges. Decorate the top with pastry leaves, brush with beaten egg or milk, and make a hole in the centre.

4 Bake the pie for 20 minutes, then reduce the oven temperature to 180°C/350°F/Gas 4. Continue to bake for 1–1¼ hours, covering the pie with foil if the pastry starts to become too brown.

Cottage Pie

INGREDIENTS

50g/2oz/4 tbsp butter
1 large onion, finely chopped
1 celery stick, finely diced
1 large carrot, finely diced
450g/1lb lean minced beef
15ml/1 tbsp plain flour
250ml/8fl oz/1 cup hot beef stock
30ml/2 tbsp chopped fresh parsley
15ml/1 tbsp tomato purée
900g/2lb floury potatoes, peeled
45-60ml/3-4 tbsp milk
10ml/2 tsp spicy brown mustard
salt and ground black pepper

SERVES 4

2 Gradually add the stock, stirring well. Stir in the chopped parsley and the tomato purée. Season well with salt and pepper. Bring to a simmer, then cover. Cook over a very low heat, stirring occasionally, for 45 minutes, until the beef is cooked and fairly dry.

3 Meanwhile, cook the potatoes in boiling salted water until they are tender. Drain well.

4 Put the potatoes in a bowl and mash them. Add the remaining butter and just enough milk to give a soft fluffy texture. Season to taste with salt and pepper. Preheat the oven to 200°C/400°F/Gas 6.

5 Stir the mustard into the beef mixture, then turn it into a baking dish. Cover with a neat layer of potato and seal to the sides of the dish. Mark with a fork. Bake for 20–25 minutes. Serve hot.

1 Melt 15g/½oz/1 tbsp butter in a frying pan over a moderately low heat. Add the onion, celery and carrot and cook until the onion is soft, stirring now and then. Add the beef and fry, stirring, until it is brown and crumbly. Sprinkle the flour evenly over the surface and stir into the meat and vegetables.

20

Poultry &
Game Pies

Curried Chicken & Apricot Pie

INGREDIENTS

30ml/2 tbsp sunflower oil
1 large onion, chopped
450g/1lb boneless chicken, roughly chopped
15ml/1 tbsp curry powder
30ml/2 tbsp apricot or peach chutney
115g/4oz/¾ cup ready-to-eat dried
apricots, halved
115g/4oz cooked carrots, sliced
5ml/1 tsp mixed dried herbs
60ml/4 tbsp crème fraîche
350g/12oz shortcrust pastry, thawed if frozen
salt and ground black pepper
beaten egg or milk, to glaze
broccoli, to serve

SERVES 6

1 Heat the oil and fry the onion and chicken until just colouring. Add the curry powder and cook briefly, then stir in the chutney, apricots, carrots, herbs and crème fraîche. Season, then transfer to a deep 1.2 litre/ 2 pint/5 cup ovenproof pie dish.

23

2 Preheat the oven to 190°C /375°F /Gas 5. Roll out the pastry to 2.5cm/1in wider than the dish. Cut a strip of pastry and press it on the dampened rim of the dish, then brush the strip with water and place the pastry lid on top, pressing to seal.

3 Trim off any excess pastry, crimp the edge, and decorate the top with pastry leaves. Brush with beaten egg or milk. Bake for 40 minutes, or until golden. Serve with broccoli.

VARIATION
Use boneless turkey instead of chicken if you wish, or even some leftovers from a roast turkey — the dark, moist leg meat is best.

Chicken, Leek & Parsley Pie

INGREDIENTS

3 skinless, boneless chicken breasts
bouquet garni, black peppercorns, onion and
carrot, for flavouring
50g/2oz/4 tbsp butter
2 leeks, thinly sliced
50g/2oz/½ cup grated Cheddar cheese
25g/1oz/¼ cup finely grated Parmesan cheese
45ml/3 tbsp chopped fresh parsley
30ml/2 tbsp wholegrain mustard
5ml/1 tsp cornflour
300ml/½ pint/1¼ cups double cream
salt and ground black pepper
beaten egg, to glaze
salad leaves, to serve
PASTRY
275g/10oz/2½ cups plain flour
pinch of salt
200g/7oz/scant 1 cup butter, diced
2 egg yolks

SERVES 4–6

1 Make the pastry. Sift the flour and salt. Blend together the butter and egg yolks in a food processor until creamy. Add the flour and process until the mixture is just coming together. Add about 15ml/1 tbsp cold water and process for a few seconds more. Knead lightly. Wrap in clear film and chill for about 1 hour.

2 Put the chicken breasts in a pan and cover with water. Add the flavourings. Poach until tender, then cool in the liquid. Cut into strips and set aside.

3 Preheat the oven to 200°C/400°F/Gas 6. Divide the pastry into two pieces, one a bit larger than the other. Roll out the larger piece on a lightly floured surface and use to line an 18 x 28cm/7 x 11in baking dish or tin. Prick the base with a fork and bake blind for 15 minutes. Leave to cool.

4 Melt the butter in a frying pan and fry the leeks over a low heat, stirring occasionally, until soft. Stir in the cheeses and chopped parsley. Spread half the leek mixture over the pastry base, leaving a border all the way round. Cover with the chicken strips, then top with the remaining leek mixture. Mix the mustard, cornflour and cream in a bowl. Season to taste. Pour over the filling.

5 Moisten the edges of the cooked pastry case. Roll out the remaining pastry and use to cover the pie. Brush with beaten egg and bake for 30–40 minutes until golden and crisp. Serve the pie hot, with salad leaves.

Greek Chicken & Feta Pie

INGREDIENTS

15ml/1 tbsp olive oil
1 onion, finely chopped
1 garlic clove, crushed
450g/1lb chopped cooked chicken
50g/2oz/⅓ cup feta cheese, crumbled
2 eggs, beaten
15ml/1 tbsp chopped fresh parsley
15ml/1 tbsp chopped fresh coriander
15ml/1 tbsp chopped fresh mint
275g/10oz filo pastry
30ml/2 tbsp olive oil
75g/3oz/¾ cup chopped toasted almonds
salt and ground black pepper
milk, to glaze
Greek feta salad, to serve

SERVES 4

1 Heat the oil and cook the onion until soft. Add the crushed garlic clove and cook for a further 2 minutes. Transfer to a bowl and add the chicken, feta, eggs and herbs. Mix thoroughly and season with salt and pepper, to taste.

2 Preheat the oven to 190°C/375°F/Gas 5. Have a damp dish towel ready to keep the filo pastry covered at all times. Cut the whole stack of filo sheets into a 30cm/12in square. Set half the filo sheets aside, covered with the towel.

3 Grease a large baking dish. Fit a filo sheet in the base. Brush it with olive oil and sprinkle with a few nuts. Repeat with the remaining available filo sheets, then  spoon in the filling and spread it evenly to the edges. Cover the pie in the same way with the reserved filo sheets, sprinkling with nuts as you go.

4 Fold in the overlapping filo edges and mark a diamond pattern on the surface of the pie with a sharp knife. Brush with milk and sprinkle on any remaining almonds. Bake for 20–30 minutes or until the pie is golden brown on top. Serve the pie with Greek feta salad.

Chicken Bouche

INGREDIENTS

450g / 1lb puff pastry, thawed if frozen
beaten egg
15ml / 1 tbsp oil
450g / 1lb / 4 cups minced chicken
25g / 1oz / 2 tbsp plain flour
150ml / ¼ pint / ¾ cup milk
150ml / ¼ pint / ⅔ cup chicken stock
4 spring onions, chopped
25g / 1oz / ¼ cup redcurrants, plus extra
to garnish
200g / 7oz / 1¾ cups button mushrooms, sliced
15ml / 1 tbsp chopped fresh tarragon, plus a
few sprigs to garnish
salt and ground black pepper
French beans, to serve

SERVES 4

1 Preheat the oven to 200°C/400°F/Gas 6. Roll out half the pastry on a lightly floured work surface to a 25cm/10in oval. Roll out the remainder to an oval of the same size and draw a smaller 20cm/8in oval in the centre using the tip of a knife.

2 Brush the edge of the first pastry shape with the beaten egg and place the other oval on top. Scallop the edge. Place on a dampened baking sheet. Cook for 30 minutes, until well risen and golden.

3 Heat the oil and fry the chicken for 5 minutes. Add the flour and cook for 1 minute. Stir in the milk and stock and bring to the boil. Add the spring onions, redcurrants and mushrooms. Cook for 20 minutes, then add the tarragon and seasoning.

4 Place the bouche on a plate, lift off the central oval and spoon in the filling. Top with the lid. Serve with French beans, garnished with redcurrants and tarragon.

27

Mixed Game Pie

INGREDIENTS

*450g / 1lb game meat, off the bone, diced
(plus the carcasses and bones)
1 small onion, halved
2 bay leaves
2 carrots, halved
a few black peppercorns
15ml / 1 tbsp oil
75g / 3oz / ½ cup rindless streaky
bacon, chopped
15ml / 1 tbsp plain flour
45ml / 3 tbsp sweet sherry or Madeira
10ml / 2 tsp ground ginger
grated rind and juice of ½ orange
350g / 12oz puff pastry, thawed if frozen
salt and ground black pepper
beaten egg or milk, to glaze
redcurrant or sage and apple jelly, to serve*

SERVES 4

1 Place the carcasses and bones in a pan, with any giblets and half the onion, the bay leaves, carrots and peppercorns. Cover with water and bring to the boil. Simmer until reduced to about 300ml/ ½ pint/1¼ cups, then strain the stock into a jug.

2 Chop the other onion half and fry in the oil until soft. Add the bacon and meat and fry quickly to seal. Sprinkle on the flour and stir until beginning to  brown. Gradually add the stock, stirring constantly as it thickens, then add the sherry or Madeira, ground ginger, orange rind and juice, and salt and pepper. Simmer for 20 minutes, until thick and flavoursome. Check the seasoning.

3 Transfer to a 900ml/1½ pint/3¾ cup pie dish and allow to cool slightly. Put a pie funnel in the centre of the filling to help hold up the pastry.

4 Preheat the oven to 220°C/425°F/Gas 7. Roll out the pastry to 2.5cm/1in larger than the dish. Cut off a 1cm/½in strip all round. Damp the rim of the dish and press on the strip of pastry. Damp the pastry strip, then lift the pastry carefully over the pie, sealing the edges at the rim. Trim off the excess pastry and scallop the edge. Decorate the top, then brush the pie with egg or milk to glaze.

5 Bake for 15 minutes, then reduce the heat to 190°C/375°F/Gas 5, for 25–30 minutes more. Serve with redcurrant or sage and apple jelly.

Farmhouse Venison Pie

INGREDIENTS

45ml/3 tbsp sunflower oil
1 onion, chopped
1 garlic clove, crushed
3 rindless streaky bacon rashers, chopped
675g/1½lb minced venison
175g/6oz/1½ cups button
mushrooms, chopped
30ml/2 tbsp plain flour
2 bay leaves
5ml/1 tsp chopped fresh thyme
450ml/¾ pint/1¾ cups beef stock
150ml/¼ pint/¾ cup ruby port
5ml/1 tsp Dijon mustard
15ml/1 tbsp redcurrant jelly
675g/1½lb potatoes
450g/1lb parsnips
1 egg yolk
50g/2oz/4 tbsp butter
freshly grated nutmeg
45ml/3 tbsp chopped fresh parsley
salt and ground black pepper

SERVES 4

1 Heat the oil in a large frying pan and fry the onion, garlic and bacon for about 5 minutes. Add the venison and mushrooms and cook for a few minutes, stirring, until browned.

2 Stir in the flour and cook for 1–2 minutes, then add the herbs, stock and port, mustard, redcurrant jelly, salt and pepper. Bring to the boil, cover and simmer for 30–40 minutes, until the meat is tender. Preheat the oven to 200°C/400°F/Gas 6.

3 Meanwhile, cut all the potatoes and parsnips into large chunks and boil these together in salted water for 20 minutes, or until tender. Drain and mash, then beat in the egg yolk, butter and nutmeg, with the chopped parsley and plenty of seasoning.

4 Spoon the meat filling into a large pie dish or four individual ovenproof dishes. Spread the potato and parsnip mixture over the meat filling in the dish or dishes. Bake a large pie for 30–40 minutes, until piping hot and golden brown. Individual pies will heat through more quickly, about 25 minutes. Serve the pie(s) at once.

Fish Pies

Classic Fish Pie

INGREDIENTS

450g / 1lb mixed raw fish, diced
finely grated rind of 1 lemon
450g / 1lb floury potatoes
25g / 1oz / 2 tbsp butter
1 egg
salt and ground black pepper
chopped fresh parsley, to garnish
SAUCE
15g / ½oz / 1 tbsp butter
15ml / 1 tbsp plain flour
150ml / ¼ pint / ¾ cup milk
45ml / 3 tbsp chopped fresh parsley

SERVES 6

1 Preheat the oven to 220°C/425°F/Gas 7. Grease a 600ml/1 pint/2½ cup ovenproof dish. Cut the fish into bite-size pieces, and place in the dish. Season and sprinkle with lemon rind. Cook the potatoes in boiling, salted water, until tender.

2 Make the sauce. Melt the butter, add the flour and cook briefly. Add the milk and whisk until thickened. Add the parsley, season and pour over the fish.

3 Drain the potatoes and mash them with the butter. Spoon the potatoes on top of the fish mixture, spread evenly and mark the top with a fork.

4 Beat the egg and brush over the potato. Bake for 45 minutes, until the top of the pie is golden brown. Sprinkle with the parsley and serve at once.

Salmon & Ginger Pie, with Lemon Thyme & Lime

INGREDIENTS

800g / 1¾lb middle cut of salmon
45ml / 3 tbsp walnut oil
15ml / 1 tbsp fresh lime juice
10ml / 2 tsp chopped fresh lemon thyme,
plus extra sprigs to garnish
30ml / 2 tbsp white wine
400g / 14oz puff pastry, thawed if frozen
50g / 2oz / ½ cup flaked almonds
3-4 pieces of drained stem ginger in
syrup, chopped
salt and ground black pepper
beaten egg, to glaze

SERVES 4–6

34

2 Divide the pastry into two pieces, one slightly larger than the other, and roll out – the smaller piece should be large enough to take two of the salmon fillets side by side and the second piece about 5cm/2in larger all round. Drain the fillets and discard the marinade.

3 Preheat the oven to 190°C/350°F/ Gas 5. Place the smaller piece of pastry on a baking sheet, then arrange two of the fillets on top. Season. Sprinkle the fish  with the almonds, ginger and a little more lemon thyme, if you like. Cover these fillets with the other two salmon fillets.

 1 Split the salmon in half, remove the bones and skin, and divide into four fillets. Mix the oil, lime juice, thyme, wine and pepper to taste, and pour over the fish in a shallow dish. Cover closely and leave the salmon to marinate overnight in the fridge.

4 Season again, cover with the second piece of pastry, tuck the edges under the pastry base and seal well. Brush with beaten egg and decorate with any leftover pastry. Bake for 40 minutes until the crust is golden. Serve on a bed of lemon thyme.

Golden Fish Pie

INGREDIENTS

675g / 1½lb white fish fillets
300ml / ½ pint / 1¼ cups milk
black peppercorns, bay leaf and onion slices,
to flavour
115g / 4oz cooked, peeled prawns, thawed
if frozen
115g / 4oz / ½ cup butter
50g / 2oz / ½ cup plain flour
300ml / ½ pint / 1¼ cups single cream
75g / 3oz / ¾ cup grated Gruyère cheese
1 bunch watercress, leaves only, chopped
5ml / 1 tsp Dijon mustard
5 sheets filo pastry
salt and ground black pepper

SERVES 4–6

I Place the fish fillets in a pan, pour over the milk and add the flavouring ingredients. Bring just to the boil, then cover and simmer for about 10–12 minutes, until the fish is just cooked through. Watch the pan closely, as milk readily boils over.

2 Lift out the fish, remove the skin and bones, then roughly flake it into a shallow ovenproof dish. Scatter the prawns over. Strain the milk and reserve.

3 Melt 50g/2oz/4 tbsp of the butter in a pan. Stir in the flour and cook for 1 minute. Stir in the reserved milk and cream. Bring to the boil, stirring, then simmer for 2–3 minutes, still stirring, until the sauce has thickened and is rich and creamy.

4 Remove the pan from the heat and stir in the Gruyère, watercress, mustard and seasoning to taste. Pour over the fish and leave to cool.

5 Preheat the oven to 190°C/375°F/ Gas 5. Melt the rest of the butter. Brush one sheet of filo pastry with butter. Crumple it loosely and place on top of the filling. Repeat with the rest of the filo sheets and butter, until they are all used up and the pie is completely covered.

6 Bake in the oven for 25–30 minutes, until the filo pastry is golden and crisp, and the filling is piping hot. Serve the pie at once. Use a large, very sharp knife to cut the pie.

Cod, Basil & Tomato Potato Pie

INGREDIENTS

1kg/2¼lb smoked cod
1kg/2¼lb white cod
600ml/1 pint/2½ cups milk
a few lemon thyme sprigs
2 basil sprigs
150g/5oz/⅔ cup butter
1 onion, chopped
75g/3oz/¾ cup plain flour
30ml/2 tbsp tomato purée
30ml/2 tbsp chopped basil
12 floury potatoes
300ml/½ pint/1¼ cups milk
salt and ground black pepper
15ml/1 tbsp chopped parsley, to serve

SERVES 8

1 Place the fish in a roasting tin with the milk and add 1.2 litres/2 pints/ 5 cups water and the herbs. Simmer for 3–4 minutes. Set aside to cool in the liquid for 20 minutes. Drain the fish, reserving the liquid. Flake the fish, removing any skin and bones.

2 Melt 75g/3oz/6 tbsp of the butter in a pan, add the onion and cook for about 5 minutes until soft but not browned. Add the flour, tomato purée and half the chopped basil. Gradually add the reserved fish poaching liquid, adding a little more milk if necessary, to make a fairly thin sauce. Bring to the boil, season with salt and pepper, and add the remaining basil. Add the fish carefully and stir gently. Pour into an ovenproof dish and set aside.

3 Preheat the oven to 180°C/ 350°F/ Gas 4. Boil the potatoes until tender. Add the rest of the butter and milk, and mash well. Stir in salt and pepper to taste and spoon on to the fish. Spread out evenly, forking to create a pattern. If you like, you can freeze the pie at this stage. Bake for 30 minutes. Sprinkle with the chopped parsley, when serving.

Vegetable Pies

Mini Spinach Pies

INGREDIENTS

25g/1oz/2 tbsp butter
1 small onion, finely chopped
175-225g/6-8oz/4-6 cups fresh or frozen
spinach, drained if frozen, chopped
2.5ml/½ tsp ground cumin
½ vegetable stock cube, crumbled
ground black pepper
milk, to glaze
PASTRY
250g/8oz/2 cups plain flour
115g/4oz/½ cup butter, chilled and diced
1 egg yolk

SERVES 10–12

1 Preheat the oven to 200°C/400°F/Gas 6. Lightly grease a muffin or patty tin.

2 Melt the butter in a saucepan, add the onion and cook gently until soft but not coloured. Stir in the spinach, then add the cumin, stock cube and pepper and cook for 5 minutes, or until the fresh spinach has wilted. Leave to cool.

3 Make the pastry. Put the flour in a bowl and rub in the butter. Add the egg yolk and enough cold water to bind. Mix to a firm dough.

4 Roll out half of the dough and cut 10–12 rounds with a 9cm/3½in cutter. Press into the tin. Add the filling, then roll out the remaining pastry and cut out  lids to cover the pies. Press the edges with a fork, to seal. Prick the tops with the fork. Brush with milk and bake for 15–20 minutes, until golden brown. Serve hot or cold.

Chestnut & Vegetable Pie

INGREDIENTS

450g/ 1lb puff pastry, thawed if frozen
450g/ 1lb Brussels sprouts, trimmed
45ml/ 3 tbsp sunflower oil
1 large red pepper, sliced
1 large onion, sliced
about 16 canned chestnuts, peeled if fresh
1 egg yolk, beaten with 15ml/ 1 tbsp water
SAUCE
40g/ 1½oz/ scant ½ cup plain flour
40g/ 1½oz/ 3 tbsp butter
300ml/ ½ pint/ 1¼ cups milk
75g/ 3oz/ ¾ cup grated Cheddar cheese
30ml/ 2 tbsp dry sherry
good pinch of dried sage
45ml/ 3 tbsp chopped fresh parsley
salt and ground black pepper

SERVES 6

1 Roll out the pastry to make two large rectangles, roughly the size of a large pie dish. The pastry should be about 5mm/¼in thick and one rectangle should be slightly larger than the other. Set the pastry aside in the fridge to rest.

2 Blanch the Brussels sprouts for 4 minutes in 300ml/½ pint/1¼ cups boiling water, then drain, reserving the water. Refresh the sprouts under cold running water, drain and set aside.

3 Heat the oil in a frying pan and lightly fry the red pepper and onion for 5 minutes. Set the pan aside until later. Cut each chestnut in half.

4 Make the sauce by beating all the flour, butter and milk together over a medium heat. Beat the sauce continuously as it comes to the boil, then stir until it is thickened and smooth. Stir in the reserved sprout water and the cheese, sherry, sage and seasoning. Simmer for 3 minutes to reduce, then mix in the chopped fresh parsley.

5 Fit the larger piece of pastry into your pie dish and layer the sprouts, chestnuts, pepper and onions on top. Trickle the sauce over the top, making sure it  seeps through to moisten the vegetables. Brush the pastry edges with the beaten egg yolk and water and fit the second pastry sheet on top, pressing the edges well to seal them securely.

6 Trim, crimp and knock up the edges, then slash the centre several times. Glaze with the egg yolk. Set aside to rest somewhere cool while you preheat the oven to 200°C/400°F/Gas 6. Bake for about 30–40 minutes, until golden brown and crisp.

Green Lentil Filo Pie

INGREDIENTS

175g/6oz/1 cup green lentils, soaked for
30 minutes in water to cover, drained
2 bay leaves
2 onions, sliced
1.2 litres/2 pints/5 cups stock
175g/6oz/¾ cup butter, melted
225g/8oz/1¼ cups long grain rice,
ideally basmati
60ml/4 tbsp chopped fresh parsley, plus a few
sprigs to garnish
30ml/2 tbsp chopped fresh dill
1 egg, beaten
225g/8oz/2 cups mushrooms, sliced
about 8 sheets filo pastry
3 eggs, hard-boiled and sliced
salt and ground black pepper

SERVES 6

1 Cover the lentils with water, then simmer with the bay leaves, one onion and half the stock for 20–25 minutes, or until tender. Season well. Set aside to cool.

2 Gently fry the remaining onion in another saucepan in 25g/1oz/2 tbsp of the butter, for 5 minutes. Stir in the rice and the rest of the stock. Season, bring to the boil, then cover and simmer for 12 minutes for basmati, 15 minutes for long grain. Leave to stand, uncovered, for 5 minutes, then stir in the fresh herbs and the beaten egg.

3 Fry the mushrooms in 45ml/3 tbsp of the butter for 5 minutes, until they are just soft. Set aside to cool. Preheat the oven to 190°C/375°F/Gas 5.

4 Brush the inside of a large, shallow ovenproof dish with more butter. Lay the sheets of filo in it, covering the base but making sure most of the filo hangs over the sides. Brush the sheets of filo well with butter as you go and overlap the pastry as required. Ensure there is a lot of pastry to fold over the mounded green lentil filling.

5 Into the pastry lining, layer rice, lentils and mushrooms, repeating the layers at least once and tucking the sliced egg in between. Season as you layer and form an even mound of filling. Bring up the sheets of pastry over the filling, scrunching the top into attractive folds. Brush all over with the rest of the butter and set aside to chill and firm up.

6 Bake the pie for about 45 minutes, until golden and crisp. Allow it to stand for 10 minutes before serving, garnished with parsley.

44

Curried Parsnip Pie

INGREDIENTS

8 baby onions, peeled
2 carrots, thinly sliced
2 large parsnips, thinly sliced
25g/1oz/2 tbsp butter
30ml/2 tbsp wholemeal flour
15ml/1 tbsp mild curry or tikka paste
300ml/½ pint/1¼ cups milk
115g/4oz/1 cup grated mature
Cheddar cheese
45ml/3 tbsp chopped fresh coriander
salt and ground black pepper
1 egg yolk, beaten with 10ml/2 tsp water
coriander or parsley sprig, to garnish
PASTRY
115g/4oz/½ cup butter
225g/8oz/2 cups plain flour
5ml/1 tsp dried thyme or oregano
cold water, to mix

SERVES 4

1 Preheat the oven to 200°C/ 400°F/ Gas 6. Make the pastry. Rub the butter into the flour until it resembles coarse breadcrumbs. Season well and stir in the thyme or oregano, then mix to a firm dough with cold water. Chill until required.

2 Boil the baby onions, carrots and parsnips in salted water for 5 minutes, then drain, reserving 300ml/ ½ pint/ 1¼ cups of the cooking liquid.

3 Melt the butter, stir in the flour and curry or tikka paste, then gradually whisk in the reserved liquid and milk, until thick and smooth. Stir in the cheese and seasoning, then add the vegetables and the chopped coriander. Pour into a pie dish, fix a pie funnel in the centre and allow to cool.

4 Roll out the pastry to 2cm/¾in larger than the top of the pie dish. Cut off a narrow strip from the pastry, brush with the egg yolk wash and fit around the rim of the dish. Brush again with egg yolk wash. Using a rolling pin, lift the rolled-out pastry over the pie top and fit over the funnel, pressing it down well on to the strips underneath. Trim the overhanging pastry and crimp the edges. Cut a hole for the funnel, decorate with pastry leaves and brush all over with the remaining egg yolk wash.

5 Bake the pie for 25–30 minutes until golden brown and crisp. Serve, garnished with a coriander or parsley sprig.

46

Spinach & Feta Pie

INGREDIENTS

900g/2lb fresh spinach, chopped
25g/1oz/2 tbsp butter or margarine
2 onions, chopped
2 garlic cloves, crushed
275g/10oz feta cheese, crumbled
115g/4oz/⅔ cup pine nuts
5 eggs, beaten
*2 saffron strands, soaked in 10ml/2 tsp
boiling water*
5ml/1 tsp paprika
1.5ml/¼ tsp ground cumin
1.5ml/¼ tsp ground cinnamon
14 sheets filo pastry
about 60ml/4 tbsp olive oil
salt and ground black pepper
Cos lettuce leaves, to serve

SERVES 6

1 Place the spinach in a large colander, sprinkle with a little salt, rub it in and leave for 30 minutes to drain the excess liquid.

2 Preheat the oven to 180°C/350°F/Gas 4. Melt the butter or margarine in a large pan and fry the onion until golden. Add the garlic, cheese and pine nuts. Remove from the heat and stir in the eggs, spinach, saffron and spices. Season with salt and pepper and mix well. Set the mixture aside.

3 Grease a large rectangular baking dish. Take seven of the sheets of filo and brush one side with a little olive oil. Place in the dish, overlapping the sheets so that the bottom is covered. Leave plenty of overhang to cover the filling later.

4 Spoon all the spinach mixture into the dish and carefully drizzle 30ml/2 tbsp of the remaining olive oil over the top. Fold the overhanging pastry over the filling. Cut the remaining pastry sheets to the size of the dish and brush each one with more olive oil. Arrange on top of the filling.

5 Brush with water to prevent curling, then bake the pie for about 30 minutes, until the pastry is golden brown. Serve warm or cold, with a salad of crisp Cos lettuce leaves.

COOK'S TIP
*Cheddar, Parmesan or any hard cheese can be
added to this dish as well as the feta.*

48

Sweet Pies

Lemon Meringue Pie

INGREDIENTS

275g/10oz/1¼ cups caster sugar
25g/1oz/2 tbsp cornflour
pinch of salt
10ml/2 tsp finely grated lemon rind
120ml/4fl oz/½ cup fresh lemon juice
250ml/8fl oz/1 cup water
3 eggs, separated
45g/1½oz/3 tbsp butter
23cm/9in pastry case, made from rich shortcrust pastry baked blind

SERVES 6

1 Combine 200g/7oz/1 cup sugar, the cornflour, salt and lemon rind in a saucepan. Stir in the lemon juice and water until smoothly blended. Bring to the boil over moderately high heat, stirring all the time. Simmer for 1 minute or until thickened.

2 Blend in the egg yolks. Cook over low heat for a further 2 minutes, stirring constantly. Remove from the heat. Add the butter and mix well.

3 Pour the lemon filling into the pastry case. Spread it evenly and level the surface. Cover closely and leave to cool completely. Preheat the oven to 180°C/350°F/Gas 4.

4 Whisk the egg whites to soft peaks. Add the rest of the sugar and continue whisking until the meringue is stiff and glossy.

5 Swirl the stiff meringue over the filling, sealing it to the rim of the pastry case. Bake for 10–15 minutes, until the meringue is golden. Serve the pie cold.

Peach Leaf Pie

INGREDIENTS

1.2kg/2½lb ripe peaches, peeled and sliced
juice of 1 lemon
90g/3½oz/½ cup caster sugar
45ml/3 tbsp cornflour
1.5ml/¼ tsp grated nutmeg
2.5ml/½ tsp ground cinnamon
1 egg beaten with 1 tbsp water, to glaze
25g/1oz/2 tbsp butter, diced
cream or ice cream, to serve
PASTRY
225g/8oz/2 cups plain flour
2.5ml/¾ tsp salt
150g/5oz/⅔ cup cold butter, cut in pieces
5-6 tbsp iced water

SERVES 8

1 Sift the flour and salt into a bowl. Rub in the butter, then stir in just enough iced water to bind the dough. Gather into two balls, one slightly larger than the other. Wrap and chill for at least 20 minutes. Preheat the oven to 220°C/425°F/Gas 7.

2 Combine the peaches with the lemon juice, sugar, cornflour and spices. Set aside.

3 Roll out the larger dough ball thinly and line a 23cm/9in pie dish. Roll out the remaining dough. Cut out 7.5cm/3in leaves. Mark with veins.

4 Brush the bottom of the pie shell with egg glaze. Add the peaches, piling them higher in the centre. Dot with the butter. Starting from the rim, cover the

peaches with concentric rings of leaves. Place tiny balls of dough in the centre, if you like. Brush with the glaze. Bake for 10 minutes. Lower the heat to 180°C/350°F/Gas 4 and bake for 35–40 minutes more. Serve hot or cold, with cream or ice cream.

Apple Pie

INGREDIENTS

675g / 1½lb cooking apples
15ml / 1 tbsp fresh lemon juice
5ml / 1 tsp vanilla essence
90g / 3½oz / ½ cup caster sugar
2.5ml / ½ tsp ground cinnamon
15ml / 1 tbsp quick-cook tapioca
20g / ¾oz / 1½ tbsp butter
1 egg yolk
10ml / 2 tsp whipping cream
PASTRY
225g / 8oz / 2 cups plain flour
5ml / 1 tsp salt
175g / 6oz / ¾ cup butter

SERVES 8

1 Make the pastry. Sift the flour and salt into a bowl. Rub in the butter, then stir in water to bind. Divide the dough into two balls, one slightly larger than the other. Roll out the larger ball thinly and line a 23cm/9in pie dish. Roll out the remaining dough. Cut out 8 large and 24 tiny leaves. Mark with veins.

2 Preheat the oven to 230°C/450°F/Gas 8. Peel the apples and slice them thinly into a bowl. Add the lemon juice, vanilla, sugar and cinnamon and toss well. Sprinkle the tapioca evenly over the bottom of the pie shell, then fill the pie shell with the apple mixture and dot with the butter.

3 Arrange the large pastry leaves in a decorative pattern on top. Decorate the rim of the pie shell with the tiny leaves. Mix together the egg yolk and cream and brush over the leaves and rim.

4 Bake the pie for 10 minutes, then reduce the heat to 180°C/350°C/Gas 4 and continue baking for 35–45 minutes, until the pastry is golden brown. Cool in the dish, set on a wire rack.

Chocolate Apricot Linzer Tart

INGREDIENTS

*350g/12oz/2 cups ready-to-eat
dried apricots
120ml/4fl oz/½ cup orange juice
175ml/6fl oz/¾ cup water
45ml/3 tbsp granulated sugar
45ml/3 tbsp apricot jam
2.5ml/½ tsp ground cinnamon
2.5ml/½ tsp almond essence
75g/3oz/½ cup chocolate chips
icing sugar, for dusting*
PASTRY
*50g/2oz/½ cup whole blanched almonds
115g/4oz/½ cup caster sugar
215g/7½oz/scant 2 cups plain flour
30ml/2 tbsp cocoa powder
5ml/1 tsp ground cinnamon
2.5ml/½ tsp salt
5ml/1 tsp grated orange rind
225g/8oz/1 cup butter, diced
30-45ml/2-3 tbsp iced water*

SERVES 10–12

1 Mix the apricots, orange juice and water in a large pan. Bring them to the boil , and simmer for 15–20 minutes, until the liquid is absorbed, stirring frequently to prevent sticking. Stir in the sugar, jam, cinnamon and almond essence, then purée in a food processor or press through a sieve.

2 Make the pastry. Process the almonds with half the sugar in the food processor, until finely ground. Sift the flour, cocoa, cinnamon and salt. Add to the processor with the remaining sugar and process to mix, then add the rind and butter and process for about 15 seconds, until mixture resembles coarse crumbs. Pulse, adding just enough iced water to make the chocolate dough stick together.

3 Knead the dough lightly. With floured fingers, press half the dough on to the bottom and sides of a 28cm/11in springform flan tin. Prick the base with a fork, then chill the pie shell. Roll out the remaining dough between two sheets of clear film to a 28cm/11in round; chill for about 30 minutes. Preheat the oven to 180°C/350°F/Gas 4.

4 Spread filling in the pie shell and sprinkle with the chocolate chips. Cut the dough round into strips and arrange a lattice over the filling. Bake for 35–40  minutes, or until top of pastry is set and the filling bubbles. Cool slightly and remove the sides of the tin. Lay strips of paper across the lattice and dust with icing sugar. Remove the paper carefully and slide the pie on to a serving plate.

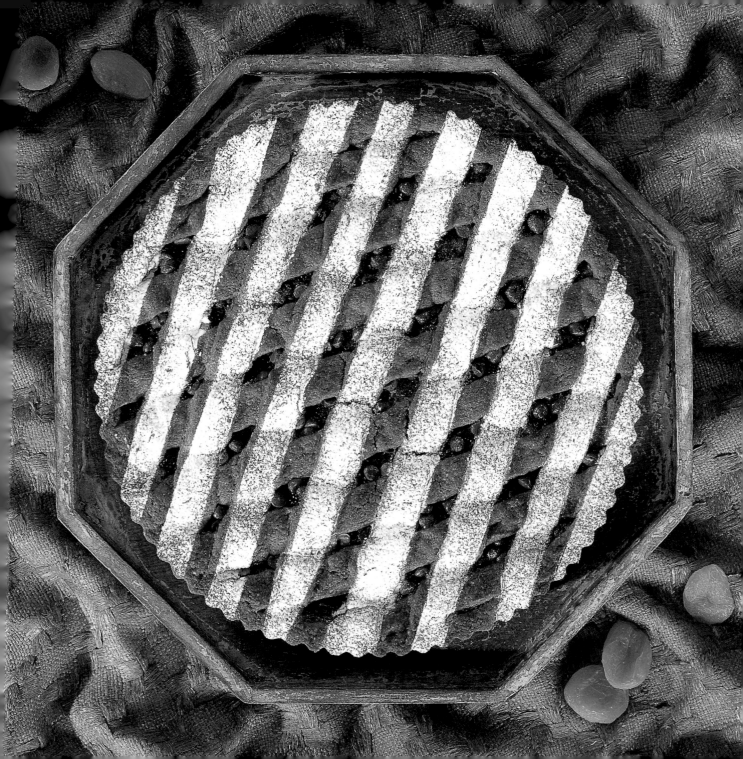

Pear & Blueberry Pie

INGREDIENTS

675g/1½lb/6 cups blueberries
30ml/2 tbsp caster sugar
15ml/1 tbsp arrowroot
2 ripe but firm pears, peeled, cored and sliced
2.5ml/½ tsp ground cinnamon
grated rind of ½ lemon
beaten egg, to glaze
caster sugar, for sprinkling
crème fraîche, to serve
PASTRY
225g/8oz/2 cups plain flour
pinch of salt
50g/2oz/4 tbsp lard, cubed
50g/2oz/4 tbsp butter, cubed

SERVES 4

1 Make the pastry. Sift the flour and salt into a bowl and rub in the fats. Stir in 45ml/3 tbsp cold water and mix to a dough. Chill for 30 minutes.

2 Place 225g/8oz/2 cups of the blueberries in a pan with the sugar. Cover and cook gently until the blueberries have softened. Press through a sieve.

3 Blend the arrowroot with 30ml/2 tbsp cold water and add to the blueberry purée. Place in a small saucepan and bring to the boil, stirring until thickened. Cool the mixture slightly.

4 Place a baking sheet in the oven and preheat to 190°C/375°F/ Gas 5. Roll out just over half the pastry on a lightly floured surface and use to line a 20cm/8in shallow pie dish or plate; do this by lopping the pastry over the rolling pin and lifting into position.

5 Mix together the remaining blueberries, the pears, cinnamon and lemon rind and spoon into the dish. Pour the blueberry purée over the top.

6 Roll out the remaining pastry to just larger than the pie dish and lay over the filling. Press the edges together to seal, then trim off any excess pastry and crimp the edge. Make a small slit in the centre to allow steam to escape. Brush with egg and sprinkle with caster sugar. Bake the pie on the hot baking sheet for 40–45 minutes, until golden. Serve warm with crème fraîche.

56

Pumpkin Pie

INGREDIENTS

25g/1oz/¼ cup pecan nuts, chopped
500g/1¼lb/2 cups pumpkin purée
475ml/16fl oz/2 cups single cream
175g/6oz/¾ cup light brown sugar
1.5ml/¼ tsp salt
5ml/1 tsp ground cinnamon
2.5ml/½ tsp ground ginger
1.5ml/½ tsp ground cloves
3.75ml/¾ tsp grated nutmeg
2 eggs
PASTRY
200g/7oz/1¾ cups plain flour
2.5ml/½ tsp salt
115g/4oz/½ cup butter
10-15ml/2-3 tbsp iced water

SERVES 8

2 On a lightly floured surface, roll out the dough to 5mm/¼in thickness. Use it to line a 23cm/9in pie dish. Trim off the excess dough.

3 Use the dough trimmings to make a decorative rope edge: cut the dough into strips and twist together in pairs. Dampen the rim of the pie shell and press on the rope edge. Sprinkle the chopped pecans over the bottom of the pie shell.

4 With an electric mixer, beat together the pumpkin purée, cream, brown sugar, salt, spices and eggs and pour the pumpkin mixture into the pie shell. Bake for 10 minutes, then reduce the heat to 180°C/350°F/Gas 4 and continue baking for about 45 minutes until the filling is set. Let the pie cool in the dish, set on a wire rack.

58

1 Preheat the oven to 220°C/425°F/Gas 7 and sift the flour and salt into a bowl. Cut in the butter, then add just enough iced water to make a firm dough.

Maple Pecan Pie

INGREDIENTS

115g/4oz/1 cup pecan halves
3 eggs, beaten
115g/4oz/½ cup dark brown sugar
150ml/¼ pint/⅔ cup golden syrup
75ml/3fl oz/6 tbsp maple syrup
2.5ml/½ tsp vanilla essence
3.75ml/¾ tsp salt
PASTRY
165g/5½oz/1⅓ cups plain flour
2.5ml/½ tsp salt
5ml/1 tsp ground cinnamon
115g/4oz/½ cup butter
30-45ml/2-3 tbsp iced water

SERVES 8

1 Preheat the oven to 220°C/425°F/Gas 7. Make the pastry. Sift the flour, salt and cinnamon into a mixing bowl. Rub in the butter until the mixture resembles coarse crumbs. Sprinkle in the iced water, 15ml/1 tbsp at a time, tossing lightly with your fingertips or a fork, until the dough clumps together and will form a ball.

2 On a lightly floured surface, roll out the dough to a circle 30cm/12in in diameter. Use it to line a 23cm/9in pie dish, easing in the dough and being careful not to stretch it. Make a fluted edge.

3 Using a fork, prick the bottom and sides of the pie shell all over. Bake for 10–15 minutes, until lightly browned. Cool, then sprinkle the pecans over the bottom of the shell. Reduce the oven temperature to 180°C/350°F/Gas 4.

4 Beat the eggs, sugar, syrups, vanilla essence and salt in a bowl. Pour over the pecans. Bake for about 40 minutes. Cool in the dish, on a wire rack.

Cherry Lattice Pie

INGREDIENTS

2 x 450g/1lb cans cherries, drained or
900g/2lb/4 cups pitted fresh cherries
75g/3oz/6 tbsp caster sugar
25g/1oz/¼ cup plain flour
25ml/1½ tbsp fresh lemon juice
1.5ml/¼ tsp almond essence
25g/1oz/2 tbsp butter or margarine
PASTRY
225g/8oz/2 cups plain flour
5ml/1 tsp salt
175g/6oz/¾ cup butter or margarine, diced
60-75ml/4-5 tbsp iced water

SERVES 8

1 Make the pastry. Sift the flour and salt into a mixing bowl. Rub in the butter or margarine until the mixture resembles coarse breadcrumbs. Sprinkle in the iced water, 15ml/1 tbsp at a time, tossing with your fingertips until the dough forms a ball.

2 Divide the dough in half and shape each half into a ball. On a lightly floured surface, roll out one of the balls to a circle about 30cm/12in in diameter.

3 Use the dough circle to line a 23cm/9in pie dish, easing the dough in and being careful not to stretch it. Trim off all the excess dough, leaving a 1cm/½in overhang around the rim. Roll out the remaining dough to 3mm/⅛in thickness. With a sharp knife, cut out 11 strips, 1cm/½in wide.

4 In a mixing bowl, combine the cherries, sugar, flour, lemon juice and almond essence. Spoon the mixture into the pastry shell and dot the butter or margarine over the surface.

5 For the lattice, space five of the pastry strips over the cherry filling and fold every other strip back. Lay a strip across, perpendicular to the others. Fold 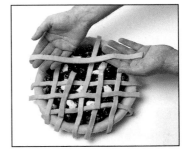 the strips back over the filling. Continue in this way, folding back every other strip each time you add a cross strip. Trim the ends of the lattice strips to make them even with the pastry overhang. Press together so that the edge rests on the pie dish rim. Flute the edge. Chill for 15 minutes. Preheat the oven to 220°C/425°F/Gas 7.

6 Bake the pie for 30 minutes, covering the edge with foil, if necessary, to prevent burning.

Mince Pies with Orange & Cinnamon Pastry

INGREDIENTS

225g/8oz/1¼ cups mincemeat
beaten egg, to glaze
icing sugar, for dusting
PASTRY
225g/8oz/2 cups plain flour
25g/1oz/¼ cup icing sugar
10ml/2 tsp ground cinnamon
175g/6oz/¾ cup butter
grated rind of 1 orange
about 60ml/4 tbsp iced water

MAKES 18

1 Sift together the flour, icing sugar and cinnamon, then rub in the butter until the mixture resembles breadcrumbs. (Pulse in a food processor, if you like.) Stir in the grated orange rind. Mix to a firm dough with the iced water. Knead lightly, then roll out to a 5mm/¼in thickness. Using a 6cm/2½in round fluted cutter, stamp out 18 circles, re-rolling the dough as necessary.

2 Using a 5cm/2in round fluted cutter, stamp out 18 smaller circles.

3 Line two muffin tins with the 18 larger circles. Place a small spoonful of mincemeat into each pastry case and top with the smaller pastry circles, pressing the edges lightly together to seal in the filling. Cut a small steam vent in the top of each pie.

4 Glaze the tops of the pies with egg and leave to rest in the fridge for 30 minutes. Preheat the oven to 200°C/400°F/Gas 6.

5 Bake the pies for 15–20 minutes, until they are golden brown. Remove them to wire racks to cool. Dust with icing sugar before serving.

Blueberry Pie

INGREDIENTS

225g/8oz/2 cups flour quantity shortcrust pastry
575g/1¼lb/5 cups blueberries
175g/6oz/¾ cup caster sugar,
plus extra for sprinkling
45ml/3 tbsp plain flour
5ml/1 tsp grated orange rind
1.5ml/¼ tsp grated nutmeg
30ml/2 tbsp orange juice
5ml/1 tsp lemon juice

SERVES 6–8

1 Preheat the oven to 190°C/375°F/Gas 5. Roll out half of the pastry and use to line a 23cm/9in pie tin that is about 5cm/2in deep.

2 Combine the blueberries, sugar, plain flour, grated orange rind and nutmeg in a bowl. Toss the mixture gently to coat all the fruit evenly. Tip the blueberry mixture into the pastry case and spread it evenly. Sprinkle over the citrus juices.

3 Roll out the remaining pastry and cover the pie. Cut out heart shapes, or cut two slits for releasing steam. Cut out small hearts from the trimmings to decorate the pie and finish the edge with a twisted pastry strip. Brush the top lightly with water and then sprinkle evenly with about 30ml/2 tbsp caster sugar.

4 Bake the pie for about 45 minutes, or until the pastry is golden brown. Serve warm or cold.

Index